AF432176

ChatBuilder

Crafting Engaging Conversations from Scratch

Loren Evers

Published by Loren Evers, 2024

While every precaution has been taken in the preparation of this book, the publisher assumes no responsibility for errors or omissions, or for damages resulting from the use of the information contained herein.

CHATBUILDER - CRAFTING ENGAGING CONVERSATIONS FROM SCRATCH

First edition. January 22, 2024.

Copyright © 2024 Loren Evers.

Table of Contents

Introduction

Welcome to "ChatBuilder: Crafting Engaging Conversations from Scratch." This book is your comprehensive guide to mastering the art of conversation, empowering you to initiate and sustain meaningful dialogues in various aspects of life. Whether you are aiming to navigate professional interactions, forge deeper personal connections, or simply enhance your conversational prowess, this book is tailored to equip you with the essential tools and strategies.

In today's fast-paced digital age, effective communication has become more crucial than ever. The ability to engage in compelling conversations holds tremendous value, facilitating success in both personal and professional spheres "ChatBuilder" is not just about exchanging words but about fostering connections that leave a lasting impact. The book aims to demystify the art of crafting engaging conversations, guiding you through practical techniques and actionable insights.

From understanding the psychology behind effective communication to navigating diverse conversational scenarios, each chapter is meticulously designed to unravel the intricacies of conversation-building. Whether you are an introvert seeking ways to comfortably engage in social situations or an extrovert aiming to refine your conversational finesse, this book caters to individuals of varying communication styles.

This book is structured to provide you with a step-by-step approach including real-life examples, and proven strategies to elevate your conversational skills. With a focus on authenticity, active listening, and adaptability, "ChatBuilder" empowers you to create conversations that captivate, connect, and leave an impression.

Join us on this transformative journey as we delve into the art of conversation-building, enabling you to construct engaging dialogues from the ground up.

This book was written using AI with extensive editing.

Each tip is short standalone chapter and is aimed to get you interested in the technique. I encourage you to practice every one of these tips and research them further using AI. This book will teach you proven techniques to start meaningful conversations and change your life.

Now let us get into it!

1. Be the First to Say Hello

Be the first to say hello. This means that you should not wait for the other person to initiate the interaction, but rather take the initiative and greet them with a confident hello. By being the first to say hello, you can demonstrate that you are approachable.

Smile: A smile is a universal sign of friendliness and warmth. It can make you and the other person feel more comfortable and relaxed. A smile can convey your cheerful outlook and mood and make the other person more receptive to your hello. You can smile and say "Hello, I am John. It is nice to meet you."

Make eye contact: Eye contact is a way of displaying your attention and respect to the other person, and it can signal your intention to start a conversation. Eye contact can help you gauge the other person's interest and reaction and adjust your hello accordingly. Make eye contact and say "Hello, how are you today?"

Use a compliment: A compliment is a way of expressing your admiration or appreciation for something about the other person, such as their appearance, behavior, or achievement. A compliment can make the other person feel good and flattered, and more likely to respond positively to your hello. Use a compliment and say "Hello, I love your dress. Where did you get it?"

Use a commonality: A commonality is something that you and the other person share, such as a location, a situation, or a preference. A commonality can help you establish rapport and connection with the other person and make your hello more relevant and personal. Use a commonality and say "Hello, I see you are reading the same book as me. What do you think of it?"

Initiating a conversation with a confident hello demonstrates that you are approachable. A smile is a universal sign of friendliness and warmth that can make you and the other person feel more comfortable and relaxed. Remember to be yourself and have fun!

2. Introduce Yourself

Introducing yourself is a way of sharing who you are, what you do, and in what interests you. It can help you establish rapport and trust with the other person. Introducing yourself can be done in different situations, such as professional events, social gatherings, or speeches. Depending on the context, adjust your introduction accordingly. Here are tips for introducing yourself in various scenarios.

In a professional setting, state your full name, your job title, and a brief description of your work. Mention something relevant to the event or the person to whom you are talking. For example, "Hi, I am John Smith, a project manager at ABC Inc. I am here to learn more about the latest trends in digital marketing. What do you do?"

In a social setting, use your first name only, and share something personal or fun about yourself. You might want to ask the other person a question to reveal your curiosity and start a conversation. Say, "Hi, I am Lisa, and I love traveling. I just came back from a trip to Italy. Have you ever been there?"

In a speech, introduce yourself by giving your name and your credentials or expertise on the topic. Share a story or a hook that relates to your speech and captures the audience's attention. Try, "Hello, everyone. I am Jane Doe, a certified financial planner, and the author of 'Money Matters.' Today, I am going to share with you the secrets of building wealth and achieving financial freedom. But before I do that, let me tell you a story about how I went from not having money to being rich in just five years."

Introducing yourself is a fantastic way to establish rapport and trust with the other person. Depending on the context, adjust your introduction accordingly. Remember, the goal of introducing yourself is to make a good impression and start a meaningful conversation. As you practice, you will become more confident and comfortable doing it.

3. Take Risks and Anticipate Success

Taking risks is an essential part of achieving your goals and living your dreams. This means stepping out of your comfort zone and trying something new or challenging. It means facing the possibility of failure or rejection, which can be scary and stressful. Taking risks can bring you many benefits, such as learning new skills, discovering new opportunities, expanding your network, and growing your confidence. You will feel more alive and excited, as you pursue your passions and purpose.

Taking risks alone is not enough. You need to anticipate success, which means expecting positive outcomes and believing in your abilities. Anticipating success can help you overcome your fears and doubts and motivate you to act. You will attract more success, as you create a positive mindset and a self-fulfilling prophecy. Anticipating success can help you cope with setbacks and failures, as you view them as temporary and valuable feedback.

Share your stories of how you took risks and achieved success, and how you learned from your failures and bounced back. You need to encourage others to take risks, anticipate success, and support them along the way.

4. Remember Your Sense of Humor

Remembering your sense of humor is a wonderful way to turbocharge your conversations and brighten your mood. Having a sense of humor means being able to laugh at yourself and the absurdities of life, and not taking things too seriously all the time. Humor can help you cope with stress, adversity, and challenges, as you find the positive aspect and the funny side of any situation. Having a sense of humor can make you more attractive, likable, and charismatic, as you spread joy and positivity to others.

A sense of humor does not mean being insensitive, rude, or offensive. Be mindful of your audience, the context, and the timing of your jokes. You need to respect the boundaries and preferences of others and avoid making fun of sensitive topics or hurting anyone's feelings. Balance your humor with empathy, compassion, and sincerity, and know when to be serious and supportive.

To enrich your life, remember your sense of humor. Cultivate your ability to laugh at yourself and the world and share your laughter with others. You need to appreciate the humor of others and join them in their laughter. Doing so, will create more fun and engaging conversations, and improve your mental and physical health.

5. Practice Starting a Conversation

Practicing diverse ways of starting a conversation is a key skill that can help you improve your communication and social confidence. Practicing diverse ways of starting a conversation helps you learn how to adapt to different situations, contexts, and audiences. You can learn how to overcome your fears, shyness, or anxiety, and become more comfortable and fluent in initiating and maintaining conversations.

There are many ways to start a conversation, depending on the purpose, the setting, and the person you want to talk to.

Asking a question: This is one of the easiest and most effective ways of starting a conversation, as it displays your interest and curiosity, and invites the other person to share their thoughts, opinions, or experiences. You can ask open-ended questions that require more than a yes or no answer, such as "What do you think of this event?" or "How do you like your job?" You can ask more specific or personal questions, such as "What are you passionate about?" or "What are your goals for this year?" You should avoid asking too many questions, or questions that are too intrusive, sensitive, or controversial, as they may make the other person uncomfortable or defensive.

Giving a compliment: This is another way of starting a conversation, as it indicates your appreciation and admiration, and makes the other person feel good. You can complement the other person on their appearance, their skills, their achievements, or their personality, such as "You have a beautiful smile" or "You are very talented" or "You are very kind." You should be sincere, specific, and genuine with your compliments, and avoid being too flattering, exaggerated, or insincere, as they may sound fake or manipulative.

Seeing: This is a way of starting a conversation, as it displays your awareness and attention, and creates a common ground with the other person. You can see the environment, the situation, the people, or the things around you, such as "It's a lovely day today" or "This place is very crowded" or "That painting is very interesting." You can see the other person, such as "You have a nice accent" or "You have a cool tattoo" or "You look familiar." You should be positive, relevant, and respectful with your observations, and avoid being negative, irrelevant, or rude, as they may offend or annoy the other person.

Telling a story: This is a way of starting a conversation, as it expresses your personality and creativity, and engages the other person's interest and emotions. You can tell a story about yourself, your experiences, your hobbies, your dreams, or your opinions, such as "I have a funny story to tell you," Or "I have an amazing experience to share with you" or "I have a strong opinion about something."

You can tell a story about someone else, such as a friend, a family member, a celebrity, or a fictional character, if it is relevant, appropriate, and entertaining. You should be clear, concise, and captivating with your stories, and avoid being boring, confusing, or misleading, as they may lose the other person's attention or trust.

Practicing different ways of starting a conversation can help you become more confident and versatile in your communication.

6. Remember People's Names

Making an extra effort to remember people's names is a valuable skill that can enhance your conversations and relationships. Remembering people's names indicates that you care about them, respect them, and value them as individuals. It helps you create a positive impression and a lasting connection with them. Remembering people's names can boost your self-confidence and social skills, as you become more comfortable and fluent in interacting with others.

Remembering people's names can be challenging, especially if you meet many people at once, or if you have a busy or distracted mind. Fortunately, there are strategies that can help you improve your memory and recall people's names more easily.

Pay attention: When you meet someone new, focus on their name and face, and avoid any distractions or interruptions. Repeat their name in your mind or aloud, and try to associate it with something memorable, such as a rhyme, a word, an image, or a person you know. If you meet someone named Mike, you can think of a bike, a spike, a microphone, or a famous Mike.

Use their name: When you talk to someone, use their name frequently in the conversation, such as in greetings, questions, compliments, or farewells. This will help you reinforce their name in your memory and make them feel more appreciated and acknowledged. You can say "Hi, Mike, nice to meet you" or "Mike, that's a great idea" or "It was a pleasure talking to you, Mike." However, do not overuse their name, as it may sound unnatural or annoying.

Write it down: After you meet someone, print their name and any details that can help you remember them, such as their appearance, their occupation, their hobbies, or their location. You can use a notebook, a phone, a business card, or a social media platform to record their name and information. You can review your notes regularly to refresh your memory and recall their name.

Ask again: If you forget someone's name, do not be afraid or embarrassed to ask them again. Most people will understand and appreciate your honesty. You can ask them politely and apologetically, such as "I'm sorry, could you please remind me of your name?" or "I apologize, I forgot your name, what was it again?" You can use a hint or a joke, such as "How do you spell your name?" or "I'm terrible with names, but great with faces."

Practice: You can practice by yourself, by reviewing your notes, by using flashcards, or by quizzing yourself. You can rehearse with others, by joining online or offline groups, clubs, or events, where you can meet new people and evaluate your memory.

Making an extra effort to remember people's names, strengthens your bonds with others. You can boost your personal and professional success, as you become more confident and charismatic in your communication.

7. If You Forgot a Person's Name

Asking a person's name if you have forgotten it is a common and understandable situation that can happen to anyone. It can be embarrassing and awkward, especially if you have met the person before or have been talking to them for a while. It is important to know how to ask a person's name if you have forgotten it in a polite and respectful way.

There are many different ways to ask a person's name if you have forgotten it, depending on the context and the relationship.

Ask them directly: This is the simplest and most honest way to ask a person's name if you have forgotten it. You can admit your mistake and apologize, and then ask them to remind you of their name. Say "I am sorry, I have a terrible memory. What was your name again?" or "I apologize, I forgot your name. Could you please tell me once more?" Most people will appreciate your sincerity and will not be offended by your question.

Ask them indirectly: This is a more subtle and discreet way to ask a person's name if you have forgotten it. You can use a hint or a joke, and then ask them to clarify their name. Say "How do you spell your name?" or "What's your full name?" or "Do you have a nickname?" or "I'm terrible with names, but great with faces." This way, you can avoid admitting that you have forgotten their name and get them to repeat or reveal their name.

Ask someone else: This is a way to ask a person's name if you have forgotten it without asking them directly. You can ask someone who knows them, such as a mutual friend, a colleague, or a host. Try "Who is that person over there?" or "What is the name of the person you were talking to?" or "Can you introduce me to that person?" This way, you can learn their name from a third party, and avoid any awkwardness or embarrassment.

Remember, the goal of asking a person's name if you have forgotten it is to express your respect and to continue a pleasant and engaging conversation with them.

8. Show Curiosity and Interest

When you show curiosity and sincere interest in others, you demonstrate that you care about them, respect them, and value them as unique individuals. You create a positive and inviting atmosphere, where the other person feels more comfortable and willing to open and share with you. Displaying curiosity and sincere interest in others can help you learn new things, discover new perspectives, and expand your horizons.

Curiosity in others does not mean being nosy, intrusive, or judgmental. Be mindful of the other person's boundaries, preferences, and feelings. You need to be genuine, authentic, and respectful with your curiosity and interest. Balance your curiosity with empathy, compassion, and appreciation.

Asking open-ended questions: These are questions that require more than a yes or no answer and invite the other person to elaborate and express their thoughts, opinions, or experiences. You can ask "What do you enjoy doing in your free time?" or "How do you feel about the current situation?" or "What are you passionate about?"

Listening actively: This means paying full attention to what the other person is saying and exhibiting that you are listening. Use verbal and non-verbal cues, such as nodding, smiling, or saying "Uh-huh" or "I see." It means reflecting what you heard, summarizing the main points, or asking clarifying or follow-up questions. "So, what I hear you saying is..." or "That sounds interesting, can you tell me more?" or "How did that make you feel?"

Expressing genuine interest: This means that you are not just pretending or being polite. You can express genuine interest by using positive and enthusiastic words, tones, and gestures, such as "Wow, that's amazing!" or "That's so cool!" or "I'm really impressed!" You can express genuine interest by relating to what they say, sharing your own experiences or opinions, or giving them a sincere compliment.

When you show curiosity and sincere interest in others, you demonstrate that you care about them, respect them, and value them as unique individuals. You create a positive and inviting atmosphere, where the other person feels more comfortable and willing to open and share with you. Displaying curiosity and sincere interest in others can help you learn new things, discover new perspectives, and expand your horizons.

9. Tell Others About Your Life

Telling others about the notable events in your life is a way of sharing your story and expressing your emotions. When you tell others about the notable events in your life, you tell them who you are, what you have experienced, and how you have grown. You invite them to connect with you on a deeper level, and to empathize with you and support you. Telling others about the momentous events in your life can help you process your feelings, gain new insights, and heal from any trauma or pain.

Telling others about your life can be challenging, especially if you are shy, introverted, or private. You may feel reluctant to open and reveal your personal details. Wait for others to ask you first. You might worry about being judged, misunderstood, or rejected, or about boring, annoying, or upsetting them with your story.

Choose the right person: Not everyone is interested or worthy of hearing your story. Choose someone who is trustworthy, respectful, and supportive of you and your life.

You need to consider the context and the timing of your conversation and avoid sharing your story with someone who is busy, distracted, or stressed.

Start with a summary: Before you dive into the details of your story, give a brief overview of what you are going to talk about, and why it is important to you. This will help you organize your thoughts and capture the attention and curiosity of the other person. "I want to tell you about the time I climbed Mount Everest. It was one of the most challenging and rewarding experiences of my life."

Use the STAR method: This is a technique that can help you structure your story in a clear and engaging way. **STAR** stands for *Situation, Task, Action,* and *Result*. Describe the situation or the event that you faced, the task or the goal that you had, the action or the steps that you took, and the result or the outcome that you achieved. You need to include the emotions or the feelings that you had along the way. "The situation was that I had always dreamed of climbing Mount Everest, but I had no experience or training. The task was to prepare myself physically and mentally for the climb, and to find a dependable guide and team. The action was that I spent six months training hard, learning the skills, and researching the best routes and seasons. The result was that I successfully reached the summit and felt an incredible sense of accomplishment and gratitude."

Ask for feedback: After you finish telling your story, ask for feedback from the other person and demonstrate that you value their opinion and perspective. You can ask them questions such as "What do you think of my story?" or "How would you feel if you were in my shoes?" or "Have you ever experienced something similar?" This will help you engage in the conversation and learn from their insights and experiences.

This tip emphasizes the importance of sharing notable events in your life as a means of self-expression and connection. It suggests that recounting such moments allows others to understand who you are, fostering empathy and support.

10. Demonstrate That You are Listening

One of the skills that can enhance your conversations and relationships is to demonstrate that you are listening by restating their comments in another way. This technique is known as paraphrasing, which means rewriting or rephrasing what was said in your own words. Paraphrasing can help you display that you are paying attention, understanding, and respecting what the other person is saying. It can help you clarify any confusion, avoid any misunderstanding, and confirm your agreement or disagreement.

Paraphrasing does not mean repeating or copying word for word. Use your own words, expressions, and examples to convey the same meaning and message. You need to be accurate, concise, and relevant with your paraphrasing, and avoid changing, adding, or omitting any valuable information or details. Balance you are paraphrasing with your own opinions, feelings, and questions, and not just rely on the other person's words.

Listen carefully: The first step to paraphrase is to listen carefully, and focus on words, tone, and body language. Avoid any distractions or interruptions and display that you are listening with verbal and non-verbal cues, such as nodding, smiling, or saying "Uh-huh" or "I see." You need to ask for clarification or repetition if you are not sure or missed something.

Identify the main points: The second step to paraphrase is to identify the main points or ideas that the other person is trying to communicate and ignore any irrelevant or redundant information. Understand the purpose, the context, and the emotion behind their message, and summarize it in your mind or aloud. You need to use your own words, expressions, and examples to restate their main points or ideas, and avoid using any jargon, slang, or technical terms that they may have used.

Check for accuracy: The third step to paraphrase is to check for accuracy and completeness of your paraphrasing, and make sure that you have not changed, added, or omitted any essential information or details. Compare your paraphrasing with the original message and see if they match in meaning and message. You need to ask for feedback from the other person and see if they agree or disagree with your paraphrasing. You can say something like "So, what I hear you saying is..." or "Let me see if I understood you correctly..." or "Did I get that right?"

When paraphrasing, remember to use your own words, expressions, and examples to convey the same meaning and message, and balance your paraphrasing with your own opinions, feelings, and questions, and not just rely on the other person's words. The technique of paraphrasing gives you another superpower in your conversational skills.

11. Communicate Enthusiasm

Communicating enthusiasm and excitement about your subjects and life in general is a way of displaying your passion and positivity to others. When you communicate enthusiasm and excitement, you demonstrate that you love what you do, what you learn, and what you experience. You create a contagious and uplifting energy, where the other person feels inspired by you and your topics. Communicating enthusiasm and excitement can help you enjoy your subjects and life more, as you focus on the positive aspects and opportunities of them.

Communicating enthusiasm and excitement does not mean being unrealistic, exaggerated, or overbearing. Be mindful of the other person's mood, and perspective. You need to be authentic, honest, and balanced with your enthusiasm and excitement. Acknowledge the challenges, difficulties, and drawbacks of your subjects and life, and not ignore or deny them.

Make it a habit to communicate enthusiasm and excitement about your subjects and life in general.

Use expressive words: The words you use can convey your enthusiasm and excitement and influence the other person's emotions and reactions. Use words that are vivid, descriptive, and powerful, and avoid words that are dull, vague, or weak. "I'm thrilled to learn about this topic" or "This is an amazing opportunity" or "I'm fascinated by this phenomenon."

Use vocal variety: The way you speak can convey your enthusiasm and excitement and capture the other person's attention. Use vocal variety, which means changing your pitch, volume, tone, and speed, and avoid speaking in a monotone, flat, or boring voice. Raise your pitch or volume to emphasize a key point, lower your tone or speed to create suspense, or modulate your voice to express different emotions.

Use body language: Your body language can convey your enthusiasm and excitement and create a connection and rapport with the other person. Use body language that is open, confident, and expressive, and avoid body language that is closed, nervous, or rigid. Smile, nod, or gesture to display your enthusiasm. You should maintain eye contact, lean forward, or use facial expressions, posture, or movements.

This tip emphasizes the importance of communicating enthusiasm and excitement about your subjects and life in general. It is a way of displaying your passion and positivity to others, which can help you enjoy your conversations and life more.

12. Meet New People

Going out of your way to try to meet new people wherever you are is a way of expanding your social circle and enriching your life. When you go out of your way to try to meet new people, you expose yourself to diverse cultures, perspectives, and experiences. You create opportunities for friendship, collaboration, and learning. Going out of your way to try to meet new people can help you overcome your shyness, loneliness, or boredom, and make you feel more connected and fulfilled.

Attempting to meet new people can be challenging, especially if you are introverted, busy, or settled in your routine. You might feel reluctant to leave your comfort zone and approach strangers. You may worry about being rejected, ignored, or misunderstood, or about wasting your time or energy on people who are not compatible with you.

Go out of your way to try to meet new people wherever you are. Explore these options and strategies.

Join online or offline groups, clubs, or events: These are places where you can find people who share your interests, hobbies, or goals, and who are looking for new connections. You can search for these groups, clubs, or events on social media, websites, apps, or newsletters, and join the ones that appeal to you. Join a book club, a hiking group, or a cooking class.

Volunteer for a cause or a project: This is a way to meet people who share your values, passions, or skills, and who are willing to contribute to something meaningful. You can look for volunteering opportunities in your area or online and sign up for the ones that match your availability and preferences. Volunteer at a local animal shelter, a soup kitchen, or a community garden.

Start a conversation with a stranger: This is a way to meet people who are in your vicinity, and who may have something in common with you or something interesting to offer. You can start a conversation with a stranger with a compliment, a question, an observation, or a joke, and then follow up with more questions or comments. You can say "I like your shirt, where did you get it?" or "What are you reading, is it good?" or "It's a beautiful day today, don't you think?" or "I'm sorry, I couldn't help overhearing, are you from around here?"

Remember, the goal of going out of your way to meet new people is to create more diverse and stimulating conversations.

13. Accept Each Person as an Individual

Accepting a person's right to be an individual with different ideas and beliefs is a way of exhibiting respect and tolerance to others. When you accept a person's right to be an individual, you acknowledge that they have their own personality, preferences, and values, and that they may differ from yours. Accepting a person's right to be an individual can help you avoid conflicts, arguments, and misunderstandings, and foster harmony, diversity, and cooperation.

Accepting a person's right to be an individual does not mean that you must agree with everything they say or do, or that you must compromise your own principles or standards. You can still have your own ideas and beliefs and express them in a civil and constructive way. You can disagree with others, and challenge their ideas and beliefs, if you do it in a respectful and polite way. You can set boundaries and limits and protect yourself from any harmful or abusive behavior.

Accept a person's right to be an individual with different ideas and beliefs by using the following methods.

Be curious: Instead of judging or dismissing others for their ideas and beliefs, try to be curious and learn more about them. Ask open-ended questions, such as "What made you think that way?" or "How did you come to that conclusion?" or "What are the benefits of that belief?"

Be empathetic: Try to put yourself in the other person's shoes and imagine how they feel and what they need. Try to see things from their point of view and appreciate their perspective. Express your empathy by using words, tones, and gestures, such as "I can see where you are coming from" or "That must be hard for you" or "I'm sorry you feel that way." This will help you connect with their emotions.

Be open-minded: Be willing to listen to and consider different ideas and beliefs and be open to changing your mind if you encounter new or better evidence. Do not assume that you know everything, or that you are always right. Be humble and admit your mistakes and be ready to learn from others. Express your openness with words, phrases, and statements, such as "I'm interested to hear your thoughts" or "I'm open to other possibilities" or "I'm willing to give it a try." This will help you expand your knowledge.

We accept each person as an individual with unique ideas and beliefs. Accepting diversity does not require agreement with all views. One can express their own opinions civilly, challenge ideas respectfully and establish boundaries. This will promote personal growth and knowledge expansion.

14. Let the Natural Person in You Come Out

Letting the natural person in you come out when talking with others is a way of being authentic and genuine in your communication. When you let the natural person in you come out, you disclose your true self, your personality, and your emotions to others. You express your thoughts, opinions, and feelings in an honest and respectful way. Letting the natural person in you come out can help you build trust, rapport, and intimacy with others, and make you more attractive, likable, and charismatic.

This does not mean that you must reveal everything about yourself, or that you must act impulsively or recklessly. Be mindful of the other person's boundaries, preferences, and feelings. You need to be appropriate, polite, and tactful with your communication. Balance your naturalness with your social skills and know when to be open and when to be discreet.

Practice skills and habits that can help you let the natural person in you come out.

Be confident: Confidence is the foundation of being natural and authentic. Be confident in yourself, your abilities, and your values, and not let others define or influence you. You need to be confident in your communication, and not be afraid or ashamed of expressing yourself. You can boost your confidence with positive affirmations, practicing self-care, and celebrating your achievements.

Be relaxed: Relaxation is the key to being natural and genuine. Be relaxed in your body, your mind, and your voice, and not be tense, nervous, or anxious. You need to be relaxed in your communication, and not be rigid, formal, or scripted. You can relax via breathing exercises, and meditation.

Be spontaneous: Spontaneity is the essence of being natural and authentic. Be spontaneous in your actions, your reactions, and your emotions, and not be predictable, boring, or dull. You need to be spontaneous in your communication, and not be hesitant, cautious, or reserved. You can be spontaneous through being curious, adventurous, and playful.

You advocate for authentic communication by expressing your true self in an honest and respectful manner. Balance naturalness with social skills while being mindful of others' boundaries. This will build trust and rapport while respecting individual preferences and feelings.

15. Tell Others What You Do

Being able to succinctly tell others in a few short sentences what you do is a way of introducing yourself and your work concisely. When you can succinctly tell others what you do, you demonstrate that you are confident, professional, and focused. You create a positive impression and a lasting connection with others. Being able to succinctly tell others what you do can help you promote your skills, achievements, and goals, and attract new opportunities and collaborations.

Telling others what you do can be challenging, especially if you have a complex, diverse, or unconventional job. It may be hard to summarize your work in a few short sentences, or to explain it in a way that others can understand and appreciate. You may worry about being too vague, too specific, or too boring with your description.

Know your audience: The first step to be able to succinctly tell others what you do is to know your audience and tailor your message accordingly. Consider who you are talking to, and what they need to know. You need to use language that is appropriate, relevant, and understandable for your audience. If you are talking to a potential employer, highlight your qualifications, experience, and achievements. If you are talking to a friend, share your passion, challenges, and aspirations.

Use the formula: The second step to be able to succinctly tell others what you do is to use a simple formula that can help you structure your message concisely. The formula is: I + verb + who/what + why/how. State who you are, what you do, who or what you do it for, and why or how you do it. "I am a graphic designer who creates logos and websites for small businesses to help them grow their online presence." or "I am a teacher who educates children in math and science to inspire them to pursue their dreams."

Add a hook: The third step to be able to succinctly tell others what you do is to add a hook that can make your message more memorable. A hook is something that can catch the attention and curiosity of your audience and invite them to ask more questions or learn more about you and your work. A hook can be a story, a statistic, a question, or a compliment. "I am a travel blogger who visits exotic destinations and writes about them on my website. Do you want to know how I got started?" or "I am a lawyer who specializes in human rights cases. I recently won a landmark case that changed the lives of thousands of people."

Sharing what you do in a conversation is essential for building stronger connections, developing self-awareness, expressing oneself, and fostering understanding among individuals.

16. Reintroduce Yourself

Reintroducing yourself to someone who is likely to have forgotten your name is a way of refreshing their memory and avoiding any awkwardness or embarrassment. When you reintroduce yourself to someone, you remind them of who you are, how you met, and what you have in common. Reintroducing yourself can help you update them on your current situation, interests, and goals, and learn more about them.

Reintroducing yourself to someone can be tricky, especially if you are not sure if they have forgotten your name, or if you have forgotten their name as well. You may feel hesitant or embarrassed to admit that you do not remember their name, or to assume that they do not remember yours.

Use a cue: A cue is something that can help you trigger the other person's memory and recognition of you and start a conversation with them. A cue can be a physical object, such as a name tag, a business card, or a souvenir. You can say "Hi, I am John, we met at the conference last month. Here is my card." A cue can be a verbal reminder, such as a reference to a previous encounter, a mutual acquaintance, or a common interest. "Hi, I am Lisa, we met at the party last week. How is your dog?"

Use humor: Humor is a way to make your reintroduction more fun and memorable, and to ease any tension or discomfort. You can use humor to acknowledge the fact that you or the other person may have forgotten each other's names, and to make light of it. "Hi, I am Mike, and I have a terrible memory. What was your name again?" or "Hi, I am Sarah, and I am sure you remember me from the karaoke night. What is your name?" However, you should be careful not to use humor that is offensive, sarcastic, or self-deprecating, as it may hurt or insult the other person or yourself.

Use a compliment: A compliment is a way to make your reintroduction more flattering and appealing, and to demonstrate your appreciation. You can use a compliment to praise the other person's appearance, skills, achievements, or personality, and to express your admiration or gratitude. "Hi, I am David, and I really enjoyed your presentation yesterday. What is your name?" or "Hi, I am Amy, and I am so glad to see you again. You have a beautiful smile. What is your name?" You should be sincere, specific, and genuine with your compliments, and avoid being too flattering, exaggerated, or insincere, as they may sound fake or manipulative.

The ability to reintroduce yourself is a critical skill in maintaining productive relationships.

17. Talk About What You Do

Being ready to tell others something interesting or challenging about what you do is a way of highlighting your skills, achievements, and passions to others. When you are ready to tell others something challenging about what you do, you indicate that you are proud, enthusiastic, and confident about your work. You create a positive impression and a lasting connection with others. Being ready to tell others about what you do can help you promote your work, attract new opportunities, and inspire others.

Telling others something interesting or challenging about what you do can be difficult, especially if you are not sure what to say, how to say it, or when to say it. You might worry about being too modest, too boastful, or too boring with your description.

Prepare in advance: The first step to be ready to tell others something interesting or challenging about what you do is to prepare in advance and have examples or stories ready to share. Think of aspects of your work that are worth telling and that may be interesting or challenging to others. "I am a web developer who creates websites and apps for various clients. One of the most challenging projects I worked on was a game app that teaches kids how to code. It was fun and rewarding to see how the kids enjoyed and learned from the app."

Use the STAR method: The second step to be ready to tell others something interesting or challenging about what you do is to use the **STAR** method, which is a technique that can help you structure your examples or stories in a clear and engaging way. *STAR* stands for *Situation, Task, Action,* and *Result*. Describe the situation or the problem that you faced, the task or the goal that you had, the action or the steps that you took, and the result or the outcome that you achieved. You need to include the emotions or the feelings that you had along the way.

"The situation was that I had to create a website for a new restaurant that wanted to attract more customers. The task was to design a website that was attractive, user-friendly, and informative. The action was that I used WordPress to create the website, and added features such as online reservation, menu, and reviews. The result was that the website increased the restaurant's online presence and boosted their sales and reputation."

Adapt to the context: The third step to be ready to tell others something interesting or challenging about what you do is to adapt to the context and the audience of your conversation, and tailor your message accordingly. You need to consider those to whom you are talking. You need to use language that is appropriate, relevant, and understandable for your audience. If you are talking to a potential employer, emphasize your skills, achievements, and goals. If you are talking to a friend, share your passion, challenges, and aspirations.

Letting others understand what you do will help you establish a lasting connection and hopefully learn new things about your friends.

18. Open and Closed Body Language

Body language is the nonverbal communication that we use to express our emotions, attitudes, and intentions. It includes our facial expressions, eye contact, gestures, posture, and movements. Body language is divided into two main categories: open and closed.

Open body language is when we expand our body and accept more space. It displays that we are confident, relaxed, and interested in the situation or the person to whom we are talking. Examples of open body language are:

Smiling and raising our eyebrows to show friendliness and curiosity.

Maintaining eye contact to show attention and respect.

Nodding and leaning forward to show agreement and interest

Uncrossing our arms and legs to show openness and receptiveness.

Using gestures and movements to show enthusiasm and excitement.

Closed body language is when we contract our body and accept less space. It indicates that we are nervous, tense, or bored in the situation or the person to whom we are talking. Here are some examples of closed body language.

Frowning and lowering our eyebrows to show displeasure and doubt.

Avoiding eye contact to show discomfort and disinterest.

Shaking our head and leaning back to show disagreement and rejection.

Crossing our arms and legs to show defensiveness and resistance.

Using minimal or rigid gestures and movements to show lack of emotion and energy.

Being aware of open and closed body language is important for effective communication and social skills. It can help us understand how others feel and what they want and influence how others perceive and respond to us.

Using open body language, we can create more positive and engaging conversations, and improve our personal and professional relationships. Avoiding closed body language, we can prevent negative and boring conversations, and avoid misunderstandings and conflicts.

19. Smile and Make Eye Contact

Smiling, making eye contact, and offering a handshake are ways to reveals that you are confident, and interested in the other person. They can help you create a positive first impression and a lasting connection.

Finding an approachable person can be challenging, especially if you are in a crowded or unfamiliar place. You may not know who is open, available, or compatible with you.

Look for cues: Cues are signs that indicate that someone is approachable and willing to talk to you. Cues can be verbal, such as saying hello, asking a question, or giving a compliment. Cues can be non-verbal, such as smiling, making eye contact, or facing you. You can look for cues in the people around you and see who is sending you positive and inviting signals. You can look for someone who is smiling and making eye contact with you, or someone who is standing alone and looking bored.

Join a group, club, or event: These are places where you can find people who share your interests, hobbies, or goals, and who are looking for new connections. You can search for these groups, clubs, or events on social media, websites, apps, or newsletters, and join the ones that appeal to you. You can join a book club, a hiking group, or a cooking class.

Start a conversation: Once you find an approachable person, to start a conversation with them, and indicate your interest and curiosity. You can start a conversation with a compliment, a question, an observation, or a joke, and then follow up with more questions or comments. "I like your shirt, where did you get it?" or "What are you reading, is it good?" or "It's a beautiful day today, don't you think?" or "I'm sorry, I couldn't help overhearing, are you from around here?"

Smiling, making eye contact, and offering a handshake are effective ways to convey confidence and interest, fostering positive first impressions and lasting connections. Practice these skills every chance you have.

20. Greet People That You See Regularly

Greeting people that you see regularly is a way of expressing your friendliness, respect, and interest in them. When you greet people that you see regularly, you acknowledge their presence, express your appreciation, and start a conversation with them. Greeting people that you see regularly can help you maintain and strengthen your relationships with them, and make you feel more connected and happier.

Greeting people that you see regularly can be boring, repetitive, or awkward, especially if you use the same greetings every time, or if you do not know what to say after the greeting. You may feel like you have nothing new or interesting to talk about, or that you are intruding on their privacy or time.

Always greet people that you see regularly in an engaging way.

Use variety: Instead of using the same greetings every time, try to use different greetings depending on the time of day, the occasion, or the mood. You can use different words, phrases, or expressions to convey your greetings, and avoid using clichés or generic greetings. Instead of saying "Hi, how are you?" every morning, you can say "Good morning, how did you sleep?" or "Hello, how's your day going?" or "Hey, what's new with you?"

Use humor: Humor is a way to make your greetings more fun and memorable, and to ease any tension or discomfort. You can use humor to tease, joke, or compliment the other person, and to make them laugh or smile. "Hi, long time no see" to someone you see every day, or "Wow, you look amazing today" to someone who is wearing casual clothes, or "Hey, are you ready for the big test?" to someone who is clearly nervous. However, you should be careful not to use humor that is offensive, sarcastic, or self-deprecating, as it may hurt or insult the other person or yourself.

Use questions: Questions are a way to indicate your interest and curiosity in the other person, and to start a conversation with them. You can use questions that are open-ended, relevant, and specific, and that invite the other person to share their thoughts, opinions, or experiences. "How was your weekend?" or "What are you working on?" or "How do you feel about the latest news?" You can use questions that are personal, creative, or hypothetical, and that challenge the other person to think or imagine. "What are you looking forward to?" or "What are you passionate about?" or "If you could travel anywhere, where would you go?"

Greeting people that you see regularly is a habit that can be cultivated and improved with time and feedback.

21. Seek Common Interest and Goals

Seeking common interest, goals, and experiences with the people you meet is a way of creating rapport, connection, and trust with them. When you seek common goals, and experiences, you demonstrate that you are curious, respectful, and interested in the other person. You find topics that you can talk about, relate to, and avoid awkward silences or conflicts. Seeking common goals and experiences can help you learn new things, discover new perspectives, and expand your horizons.

Seeking common interest, goals and experiences can be challenging, especially if you do not know much about the other person, or if you have quite divergent backgrounds, cultures, or personalities. It might be hard to find something that you have in common, or to express it in a way that the other person can appreciate. You might worry about being boring, intrusive, or insensitive with your questions or comments.

Use open-ended questions: These are questions that require more than a yes or no answer and invite the other person to elaborate and express their thoughts, opinions, or experiences. You can use open-ended questions to explore the other person's interests, goals, and experiences, and to find out what you have in common. "What do you enjoy doing in your free time?" or "What are you working on right now?" or "What are some of the most memorable experiences you've had?"

Use active listening: This means paying full attention to what the other person is saying and showing that you are listening with verbal and non-verbal cues, such as nodding, smiling, or saying "Uh-huh" or "I see." It means reflecting what you heard, summarizing the main points, or asking clarifying or follow-up questions. "So, what I hear you saying is…" or "That sounds interesting, can you tell me more?" or "How did that make you feel?"

Use common ground: This means finding and emphasizing the things that you have in common with the other person. You can use common ground to present your agreement, appreciation, and empathy with the other person, and to build rapport and trust with them. "I can relate to that, I had a similar experience" or "I agree with you, I think the same way" or "You are not alone, I feel the same way."

Seeking common goals will enable you to deepen conversation and establish a bond with people you meet.

22. Make an Effort to Help People

Trying to help people if you can be a way of demonstrating your kindness, generosity, and compassion to others. When you try to help people, you demonstrate that you care about them, their problems, and their well-being. You create a positive impact and a lasting difference in their lives. Trying to help people can help you feel more fulfilled, grateful, and happy.

Trying to help people can be challenging, especially if you are not sure how to help, who to help, or when to help. You may find it hard to offer your help in a way that is appropriate, effective, and respectful.

Make a concerted effort to help people if you can.

Volunteer your time: This is a way to help others in your community or beyond, giving your time and skills to a cause or a project that you care about. You can look for volunteering opportunities in your area or online and sign up for the ones that match your availability and preferences.

Volunteer at a local animal shelter, a soup kitchen, or a community garden.

Donate your resources: This is a way to help others in need, though giving your money or goods to a charity or a nonprofit organization that you trust and support. You can research the best charities or nonprofits that align with your values and goals and donate as much as you can afford or spare. Donate to a food bank, a disaster relief fund, or a scholarship program.

Offer your support: This is a way to help others in your personal or professional network, by offering your emotional, practical, or professional support to them. You can reach out to the people you know who are going through a tough time, and offer your listening ear, your advice, or your assistance. Offer to listen to a friend who is feeling depressed, to help a colleague who is struggling with a project, or to mentor a student who is looking for a career path.

Trying to help others is a means of expressing kindness, generosity, and compassion. You need to make a concerted effort to deepen this skill. The more you do it the easier it will become.

23. Let Others Play the Expert

Letting others play the expert is a way of expressing your respect, appreciation, and curiosity to others. When you let others play the expert, you display that you value their knowledge, skills, and experience, and that you want to learn from them. You create a positive and inviting atmosphere, where the other person feels more comfortable and confident to share with you.

Letting others play the expert does not mean that you must be passive, ignorant, or submissive. You can still have your own opinions, questions, and contributions, and express them in a civil and constructive way. You can challenge others, and ask for evidence or clarification, if you do it in a respectful and polite way. You can set boundaries and limits and protect yourself from any false or harmful information.

Ask open-ended questions: These are questions that require more than a yes or no answer and invite the other person to elaborate and explain their thoughts, opinions, or experiences. You can ask open-ended questions to explore the other person's expertise, and to present your interest and curiosity. Ask "How did you learn to do that?" or "What are the benefits of that method?" or "What are some of the challenges or opportunities in that field?"

Give positive feedback: This means giving the other person praise, appreciation, or gratitude for their expertise, and for sharing it with you. You can give positive feedback using words, tones, and gestures, such as "Wow, that's impressive!" or "That's very helpful, thank you!" or "I'm really impressed by your skills!" You can give positive feedback relating to what they say, sharing your own experiences or opinions, or giving them a sincere compliment. Say "I can relate to that, I had a similar experience" or "I agree with you, I think the same way" or "You are very talented, I admire your skills."

Ask for advice or help: This means asking the other person for their suggestions, recommendations, or assistance on something that you need or want to do. You can ask for advice or help being specific, polite, and humble, and by explaining why you need or want their expertise. You can show your gratitude and willingness to follow their advice or help. "I'm having trouble with this project, can you give me some tips?" or "I'm interested in learning more about this topic, can you recommend me some resources?" or "I'm looking for a new career path, can you help me with some options?"

Letting others play the expert can help you gain new insights, perspectives, and opportunities.

24. Answering Common Questions

Be open to answering common ritualistic questions. These are questions that people often ask to initiate or maintain a social interaction, such as "How are you?" "What do you do?" "Where are you from?" and so on. These questions may seem trivial or boring, but they serve a purpose of establishing rapport and showing interest in the other person.

Answering these questions honestly and enthusiastically, creates a positive impression and invites further conversation. You can use these questions as an opportunity to share something interesting or unique about yourself, or to ask a follow-up question to the other person.

If someone asks you "What do you do?" you can say "I am a writer working on a book about ways to create engaging conversations. What about you?" This way, you can turn a common ritualistic question into a meaningful exchange.

25. Be Enthusiastic About Other People

We all have those things that light us up, hobbies that make our eyes sparkle and send shivers of excitement down our spines. But have you ever stopped to consider the magic that happens when you embrace the passions of others with the same fervor you reserve for your own? It is a skill worth cultivating, for it unlocks a treasure trove of connection, understanding, and shared joy.

Here is why being enthusiastic about other people's interests is a superpower.

Building Bridges: Imagine two strangers, Sarah, the bookworm, and Alex, the adrenaline junkie. On the surface, they seem like opposites. But when Sarah listens with rapt attention as Alex describes his latest rock-climbing feat, and Alex loses himself in Sarah's enthusiastic analysis of a classic novel, a bridge is built. Shared enthusiasm, even for something outside your own realm, fosters connection and creates a sense of mutual respect.

Expanding Your World: Every person's passion is a portal to a universe you might never have explored. Approaching someone's interest with genuine curiosity, you open yourself up to new knowledge, perspectives, and experiences. Who knows? You might just discover a hidden talent for pottery after attending a friend's ceramics class or develop a newfound appreciation for birdwatching after accompanying your dad on an early morning trek.

The Gift of Validation: There is nothing quite like the feeling of someone being genuinely excited about something you love. It validates your passion, boosts your confidence, and makes you feel seen and understood. Revealing enthusiasm for others gifts them a little dose of joy and encouragement, strengthening the bond between you.

Remember, being enthusiastic does not require becoming an expert in someone else's field. It is simply about asking thoughtful questions and celebrating their passion with them. So, the next time someone starts talking about their love for underwater basket weaving or competitive yo-yoing, put on your curiosity hat, lean in, and let the sparks fly! You might just surprise yourself with what you discover, both about them and about your own capacity for connection.

Here are additional tips for cultivating enthusiasm:

Ask open-ended questions: Instead of a simple "how was it?", dig deeper with "what was your favorite part?" or "what surprised you the most?".

Connect it to your own experiences: Share a relevant anecdote or a similar interest you have. This shows you are actively listening and finding common ground.

Offer encouragement: If someone is nervous about their passion, express your belief in them and their abilities. A little cheer can go a long way.

Be present: Put away your phone, make eye contact, and give your full attention to the person who is sharing their passion.

Embracing the thrill of other people's passions, opens you up to a richer, more fulfilling world. So, go forth, be the cheerleader, the curious explorer, and watch the connections bloom!

26. Giving and Receiving Information

This means that you should not dominate the conversation by talking too much or too little, but rather share the floor equally with the other person.

Pausing after you make a point or tell a story and inviting the other person to comment or ask a question.

Asking for the other person's opinion, feedback, or experience on the topic you are discussing.

Acknowledging what the other person says and building on it with your own thoughts or questions.

Switching the topic when the conversation is losing steam, and finding something new that both of you like.

Ending the conversation gracefully when it reaches a natural conclusion and expressing your appreciation for the other person's time and attention.

A balanced conversation is more enjoyable, respectful, and engaging for both parties.

27. Speak About a Variety of Topics

This means that you should have general knowledge and curiosity about the world and be able to discuss different things with different people. Being able to speak about a variety of topics and subjects, reveals that you are well-informed, open-minded, and adaptable, and find common ground and interests with the other person.

Reading books, articles, blogs, magazines, or newsletters that cover a wide range of topics, from science and technology to arts and culture.

Watching documentaries, podcasts, TED talks, or YouTube videos that explore various aspects of the world, such as history, geography, psychology, or philosophy.

Learning new skills, hobbies, languages, or facts that can enrich your mind and expand your horizons.

Asking questions and listening to the answers when you meet someone who has a different background, perspective, or expertise than you.

If you can speak on a variety of topics, you become an interesting person to talk to and can easily find common points of interest. Practice this skill!

28. Keep Up on Current Events

You should be aware of what is happening in the world and have opinions or perspectives on them. Keeping up to date on current events and issues, demonstrates that you are engaged, and informed in the world around you. Always be prepared with relevant and timely topics to talk about with people.

Following reliable and diverse news sources, such as newspapers, websites, podcasts, or social media, which cover local, national, and international news.

Discussing current events and issues with your friends, family, colleagues, or online communities, and listening to their views and arguments.

Researching more about the topics that interest you, and finding out the facts, causes, effects, and solutions of the problems or challenges facing the world.

Respecting the opinions and beliefs of others, even if they differ from yours, and avoiding heated or offensive arguments.

Just like speaking about a variety of topics, knowing even a small amount about current events will help you find common connections with the people you interact with.

29. Express Your Feelings and Opinions

Be willing to express your feelings, opinions, and emotions to others. This means that you should not be afraid or ashamed to share what you think, feel, or want, and to be honest and authentic with the other person. Expressing your feelings, opinions, and emotions to others, reveals that you are confident, vulnerable, and human, and create a deeper connection and trust with the other person.

Using "I" statements, such as "I feel…," "I think…," "I want…," to communicate your perspective and needs clearly and respectfully.

Avoiding judgmental, blaming, or aggressive language, such as "You always…," "You never…," "You should…," that can make the other person defensive or angry.

Sharing positive feelings, opinions, and emotions, such as gratitude, appreciation, admiration, or joy, as well as negative ones, such as sadness, anger, frustration, or fear, and explaining why you feel that way.

Respecting the feelings, opinions, and emotions of others, even if they differ from yours, and listening to them with empathy and compassion.

You must be open in expressing your emotions and viewpoints to others. This skill will make you authentic and will foster confidence and a deeper connection with others.

30. Enjoying Your Conversation

Visually show others that you are enjoying your conversation with them. This means that you should use your body language, facial expressions, and gestures to convey your attention, and enthusiasm. Visually showing others that you are enjoying your conversation with them, makes them feel more comfortable, confident, and valued, and encourage them to continue the interaction.

Nod: Nodding is a way of showing your agreement, understanding, and encouragement to the other person, and it can signal that you are listening and following the conversation. Nodding can help you maintain eye contact and avoid looking away or distracted. Nod and say "Yes, I agree" or "I see what you mean" or "That's interesting."

Lean: Leaning is a way of showing your involvement, curiosity, and attraction to the other person, and it can reduce the physical distance and create a sense of intimacy. Leaning can help you focus on the conversation and avoid any external distractions. Lean forward and say, "Tell me more" or "How did you do that?" or "You are so funny."

Smile: Smiling is a way of showing your happiness, warmth, and friendliness to the other person, and it can make you and the other person feel more relaxed and positive. Smiling can convey your appreciation and gratitude for the conversation and the other person. Smile and say, "I'm glad you said that" or "Thank you for sharing that" or "I enjoy talking to you."

Life is short, there is no reason that you should not enjoy your conversations. It should not even be necessary to practice this skill, it should be part of your inner self.

31. Invite Others to Join

Be ready to issue invitations to others to join you for other events or activities to further the relationship. This means that you should not end the conversation abruptly or without a follow-up, but rather suggest or propose something that you and the other person can do together in the future. Issuing invitations to others creates opportunities for more conversations and interactions.

Use a compliment: A compliment is a way of expressing your admiration or appreciation for something about the other person, such as their personality, skills, or achievements. A compliment can make the other person feel good and flattered, and more likely to accept your invitation. Utilize a compliment and say "You are so fun to talk to. Would you like to hang out with me sometime?" or "You are so talented. I would love to see your work. Can I visit your studio?" or "You are so knowledgeable. I would love to learn more from you. Can I join your book club?"

Use a commonality: A commonality is something that you and the other person share, such as a hobby, a goal, or a preference. A commonality can help you establish rapport and connection with the other person and make your invitation more relevant and personal. Employ a commonality and say "We both love hiking. Do you want to go to the national park with me next weekend?" or "We both have the same fitness goal. Do you want to join me for a yoga class tomorrow?" or "We both enjoy the same music genre. Do you want to go to the concert with me next month?"

Use a suggestion: A suggestion is a way of offering or recommending something that you think the other person might like or benefit from, such as a place, a service, or a product. A suggestion can indicate that you are helpful, thoughtful, and attentive, and that you have paid attention to the conversation and the other person's needs or interests. Utilize a suggestion and say "There is a high-quality restaurant nearby that serves your favorite cuisine. Do you want to try it with me?" or "There is a new movie that I think you would love. Do you want to watch it with me?" or "There is a sale at the store that has the item you wanted. Do you want to go shopping with me?"

Inviting others to become involved in your conversations creates a participatory environment, fostering collaboration, diverse perspectives, and building functional relationships, contributing to the success of the endeavor.

32. Keep in Touch with Friends

Find ways to stay connected with friends and acquaintances you meet. This means that you should not lose contact or connection with the people you have had an enjoyable conversation with, but rather follow up and maintain the relationship. Finding ways to stay connected with friends and acquaintances, demonstrates that you are caring, dependable, creates more opportunities for future interactions.

Exchange contact information: This is the most basic and essential way of staying connected with someone, and it involves exchanging your phone number, email address, social media account, or any other means of communication. You can exchange contact information at the end of the conversation, or during the conversation if it is relevant and natural. "Can I have your number? I would love to chat with you again" or "Do you have Instagram? I would love to see your photos" or "Can I email you? I have resources that might interest you."

Send a follow-up message: This is a way of expressing your appreciation and interest for the conversation, and it involves sending a message to the other person shortly after the conversation, or within a reasonable time limit. You can send a follow-up message to thank the other person, to give them feedback, to share something related to the conversation, or to invite them for another conversation. "Thank you for the enjoyable conversation. I really enjoyed it" or "I tried your recommendation, and it was amazing. Thank you for the tip" or "I found this article that you might like. It is about the topic we discussed" or "I had a lot of fun talking to you. Do you want to talk again soon?"

Stay in touch regularly: This is a way of maintaining and strengthening the relationship, and it involves staying in touch with the other person on a regular basis, depending on the level and nature of the relationship. You can stay in touch regularly sending messages, making calls, or meeting in person, sharing your thoughts, feelings, experiences, or interests. "How are you doing? I hope you are well" or "I saw this movie and I thought of you. Have you seen it?" or "I miss you. When can we meet again?" or "I have exciting news to tell you. Can I call you?"

Staying connected with friends is essential for several reasons, as it can increase your sense of belonging and purpose, boost happiness, reduce stress, and improve self-confidence.

33. Seek Out Others' Opinions

You should not only express your own thoughts and views but ask for and listen to the thoughts and views of the other person. Seeking out others' opinions, shows that you are respectful, curious, and open-minded, and learn something new and different from the other person.

Ask open-ended questions: These are questions that require more than a yes or no answer and invite the other person to elaborate and explain their opinions. You can ask open-ended questions to explore the other person's perspective, and to reveal your curiosity. "What do you think of this issue?" or "How do you feel about this situation?" or "What are your reasons for this choice?"

Use active listening: This means paying attention to what the other person is saying and showing that you are listening and understanding. You can use active listening to acknowledge and validate the other person's opinions, and to encourage them to share more with you. You can use active listening by nodding, making eye contact, paraphrasing, summarizing, or giving feedback. "I see what you mean" or "That's an interesting point" or "I agree with you on that" or "I have a different opinion on that."

Respect differences: This means accepting and appreciating that the other person may have different opinions from yours, and that they have the right to have them. You can respect differences by avoiding judgment, criticism, or argument, and being polite and civil. You can respect differences by trying to understand the other person's point of view and finding common ground or areas of agreement. "I respect your opinion, even though I don't share it" or "I can see where you are coming from, but I have a different perspective" or "We may disagree on this, but we can agree on that."

Seeking out others' opinions is valuable as it reflects the character strengths of wisdom and humility, allowing individuals to interpret the complex world in diverse ways. It provides the opportunity to gain different perspectives, fostering learning, improvement, and fresh thinking.

34. Look for the Positive

One of the most beneficial ways to fuel a conversation is to look for the positive in those you meet. This means that you should not focus on the flaws, faults, or mistakes of the other person, but rather on their strengths, virtues, or achievements. Looking for the positive in those you meet, presents that you are optimistic, supportive, and appreciative, and inspire and motivate the other person.

Utilize a compliment: A compliment is a way of expressing your admiration or appreciation for something about the other person, such as their appearance, behavior, or accomplishment. A compliment can make the other person feel good and flattered, and more likely to respond positively to your conversation. "You have a beautiful smile" or "You are very kind" or "You did a great job."

Use a gratitude: A gratitude is a way of expressing your thankfulness or recognition for something that the other person has done for you or for others. A gratitude can make the other person feel valued and respected, and more likely to reciprocate your kindness. Use a gratitude and say, "Thank you for your help" or "Thank you for your time" or "Thank you for your generosity."

Use a curiosity: A curiosity is a way of expressing your eagerness to learn more about the other person, such as their background, hobbies, or goals. A curiosity can make the other person feel important and interesting, and more likely to share more with you. Use a curiosity and say, "What do you do for fun?" or "What are you passionate about?" or "What are your dreams?"

Actively seeking the positive has numerous benefits, including increased life span, lower rates of depression and enhanced quality of life. Always stay positive, it is infectious and will make people love to have conversations with you.

35. Start and End Your Conversations Right

Start and end your conversations with the person's name and a handshake or warm greeting. This means that you should use the person's name when you greet them and when you say goodbye, and offer a physical gesture of respect and friendliness, such as a handshake, a hug, or a kiss on the cheek. Starting and ending your conversations with the person's name and a handshake or warm greeting, displays that you are attentive, polite, and personal, and make an impression on the other person.

Remember their name: This is the most basic and essential way of starting and ending a conversation with someone, and it involves remembering and using their name correctly and appropriately. You can remember their name by repeating it when you first meet them, associating it with something familiar, or writing it down. You can use their name saying it clearly and confidently and using the appropriate title or formality. "Hello, Mr. Smith. It is a pleasure to meet you" or "Goodbye, Sarah. It was nice talking to you."

Use a handshake: This is the most common and universal way of starting and ending a conversation with someone, and it involves offering and accepting a firm and brief grip of the hand. You can use a handshake to solidify your respect, confidence, and professionalism, and to establish physical contact and rapport. You can say "Hello, John. I am Lisa. Nice to meet you" and shake their hand, or "Goodbye, John. Thank you for your time" and shake their hand again.

Use a warm greeting: This is a more personal and intimate way of starting and ending a conversation with someone, and it involves offering and accepting a hug, a kiss, or a cheek-to-cheek touch. You can use a warm greeting to indicate your affection, friendliness, and familiarity, and to create a sense of closeness and connection. "Hello, Maria. I am so happy to see you" and hug them, or "Goodbye, Maria. Take care" and kiss them on the cheek.

Practice starting and ending conversations. Leaving a conversation on a positive note will make people want to talk to you in the future.

36. Be Friendly with Your Neighbors

One of the most rewarding ways to encourage a conversation is to take the time to be friendly with your neighbors and coworkers. This means that you should not ignore or avoid the people you live or work with, but rather greet them, chat with them, and help them when you can. Taking the time to be friendly with your neighbors and coworkers, shows that you are sociable, considerate, and cooperative, and build trust and rapport with them.

Say hello and goodbye: This is the most basic and effortless way of being friendly with your neighbors and coworkers, and it involves acknowledging their presence and saying hello when you see them, and goodbye when you leave. You can say hello and goodbye using their name, smiling, waving, or nodding. "Hello, Bob. How are you today?" or "Goodbye, Alice. Have a nice evening."

Make small talk: This is a way of being friendly with your neighbors and coworkers, and it involves having a casual and brief conversation with them about topics that are not too personal or controversial, such as the weather, the news, or the weekend plans. Make small talk by asking questions, giving compliments, or sharing anecdotes. "How do you like the new coffee machine?" or "You look great today. Is that a new haircut?" or "I went to the park with my kids yesterday. It was so much fun."

Offer help or support: This is a way of being friendly with your neighbors and coworkers, and it involves offering or aiding or encouragement to them when they need it or appreciate it. You can offer help or support noticing their needs, expressing your willingness, or giving your advice. "Do you need a hand with that?" or "I'm here if you need anything" or "You did a great job on that presentation."

Being friendly to your neighbors fosters a sense of community, enhances safety, and provides a support system in times of need. This is a skill you must practice.

37. Get to Know People Better

Let others know that you would like to get to know them better. This means that you should not be shy or hesitant to express your interest and curiosity in the other person, and to invite them to share more about themselves. Letting others know that you would like to get to know them better, you can reveal that you are open, attentive, and genuine, and create a deeper connection and trust with them.

Use a compliment: A compliment is a way of expressing your admiration or appreciation for something about the other person, such as their personality, skills, or achievements. A compliment can make the other person feel good and flattered, and more likely to open to you. Use a compliment and say "You have a profound sense of humor. I would love to hear more of your jokes" or "You have a lot of wisdom. I would love to learn from you" or "You have a lot of courage. I would love to hear your story."

Use a curiosity: A curiosity is a way of expressing your interest or eagerness to learn more about the other person, such as their background, hobbies, or goals. A curiosity can make the other person feel important and interesting, and more likely to share more with you. Use a curiosity and say, "What do you do for fun?" or "What are you passionate about?" or "What are your dreams?"

Use a suggestion: A suggestion is a way of offering or recommending something that you think the other person might like or benefit from, such as a place, a service, or a product. A suggestion can show that you are helpful, thoughtful, and attentive, and that you have paid attention to the conversation and the other person's needs or interests. You can use a suggestion and say "There is an excellent restaurant nearby that serves your favorite cuisine. Do you want to try it with me?" or "There is a new movie that I think you would love. Do you want to watch it with me?" or "There is a sale at the store that has the item you wanted. Do you want to go shopping with me?"

Getting to know people better is essential for building meaningful connections that provide support, enhance well-being, and offer opportunities for personal and professional growth.

38. Ask About Previous Conversations

One of the most respectful and attentive ways to start a conversation is to ask others about things that they have told you in previous conversations. This means that you should not forget or ignore the information that the other person has shared with you before, but rather recall and follow up on it. Asking others about things that they have told you in previous conversations, illustrates that you are caring, and loyal, and strengthens the relationship.

Use a reminder: This is a way of refreshing the memory of the previous conversation, and it involves mentioning the topic, the date, or the context of the conversation. You can use a reminder to show that you have paid attention and remembered the details, and to avoid confusion or repetition. "Last week, you told me that you were going to a job interview. How did it go?" or "The last time we talked, you mentioned that you were having trouble with your car. Did you fix it?" or "Remember when we discussed that book you were reading? What did you think of the ending?"

Use a follow-up question: This is a way of showing your curiosity and concern for the other person, and it involves asking a question that relates to the previous conversation. You can use a follow-up question to explore the other person's feelings, opinions, or experiences, and to demonstrate your empathy. "How are you feeling after your surgery?" or "What did you learn from your trip to Italy?" or "How do you cope with your stress?"

Use feedback: This is a way of showing your appreciation and support for the other person, and it involves giving a comment or a compliment that relates to the previous conversation. You can use feedback to acknowledge and validate the other person's achievements, efforts, or challenges, and to express your respect and admiration. "I am so proud of you for getting that promotion. You deserve it" or "I am so impressed by your skills. You are amazing" or "I am so sorry for your loss. You are strong."

Asking about previous conversations when speaking to people enhances communication by demonstrating active listening, building rapport, and fostering a deeper understanding of the individual's thoughts and experiences.

39. Listen Carefully for Free Information

One of the most useful ways to encourage conversation is to listen carefully for free information. This means that you should pay attention to the details, facts, or clues that the other person gives you during the conversation, without you asking for them. Listening carefully for free information, demonstrates that you are observant, and finds topics or questions to continue the conversation.

Use active listening: This means paying attention to what the other person is saying and showing that you are listening and understanding. You can use active listening to identify and remember the free information that the other person gives you, and to encourage them to give you more. You can use active listening by nodding, making eye contact, paraphrasing, summarizing, or giving feedback. "I see what you mean" or "That's an interesting point" or "I agree with you on that."

Use follow-up questions: This means asking questions that relate to the free information that the other person has given you, and that invite them to elaborate and explain more. You can use follow-up questions to show your curiosity and concern for the other person, and to keep the conversation going. Say "How did you get into that hobby?" or "What are the benefits of that method?" or "What are some of the challenges or opportunities in that field?"

Use feedback: This means giving a comment or a compliment that relates to the free information that the other person has given you, and that expresses your appreciation or admiration. You can use feedback to acknowledge and validate the other person's information, and to make them feel good and valued. "That's amazing" or "That's very helpful" or "You are so talented."

Listening carefully for free information during conversations is advantageous as it enhances understanding, strengthens relationships, and provides valuable insights that contribute to effective communication and decision-making.

40. Ask Open-Ended Questions

Be ready to ask open-ended questions to learn more. This means that you should not only ask questions that can be answered with a yes or no, but questions that invite the other person to share their thoughts, feelings, or experiences. Asking open-ended questions, reveals that you are curious, and discovers new and interesting things about the other person.

Start with "how," "why," or "what": These are the most familiar words that begin open-ended questions, and they can help you explore the other person's perspective, motivation, or preference. For example, you can ask "How do you feel about that?" or "Why did you choose that?" or "What do you think of that?"

Use follow-up questions: These are questions that relate to the previous answer, and that invite the other person to elaborate or explain more. You can use follow-up questions to show your attention and understanding, and to keep the conversation going. You can ask "Can you tell me more about that?" or "How did that happen?" or "What did you learn from that?"

Avoid leading or loaded questions: These are questions that imply or suggest a certain answer, or that have a hidden agenda or bias. You should avoid leading or loaded questions, as they can make the other person feel pressured, manipulated, or offended. You should avoid asking "Don't you think that's wrong?" or "Why are you so lazy?" or "What's wrong with you?"

Asking open-ended questions during conversation is crucial for fostering deeper engagement, encouraging thoughtful and detailed responses, and promoting meaningful communication.

41. Change the Topic When Needed

Know when and how to change the topic of conversation when it has run its course. This means that you should be able to sense when the conversation is losing steam, becoming boring, or going nowhere, and then switch to a different topic that is more relevant, interesting, or productive. Changing the topic of conversation when it has run its course, reveals that you are flexible, adaptable, and creative, and keep the conversation flowing and engaging.

Use a transition: This is a way of signaling that you want to move on to a new topic, and it involves using a word, a phrase, or a sentence that connects the old topic to the new one. You can use a transition to be respectful and polite, and to avoid abrupt or awkward changes. Say "Speaking of that..." or "By the way..." or "That reminds me of something..."

Use a question: This is a way of introducing a new topic, and it involves asking the other person a question that relates to the new topic. You can use a question to disclose that you are curious, and to invite the other person to join the new topic. "What do you think of the new policy?" or "How do you feel about the upcoming event?" or "What are your plans for the weekend?"

Use a suggestion: This is a way of proposing a new topic, and it involves offering or recommending something that you think the other person might like or benefit from, such as a place, a service, or a product. You can use a suggestion to show that you are helpful, thoughtful, and attentive, and to spark the other person's interest or curiosity. "Have you tried the new restaurant in town?" or "Have you seen the latest movie?" or "Have you heard about the new app?"

Changing the topic during conversations is valuable as it allows for flexibility, maintains engagement, and helps navigate discussions to be more comfortable or relevant subjects, enhancing overall communication dynamics.

42. Get People Excited

Searching for the things that really get another excited, makes them feel valued and respected, and learn something new and different from them.

Use open-ended questions: These are questions that require more than a yes or no answer and invite the other person to elaborate and explain their thoughts, feelings, or experiences. You can use open-ended questions to explore the other person's passions, and to show your interest and curiosity. "What do you love to do?" or "What makes you happy?" or "What are you most proud of?"

Use active listening: This means paying attention to what the other person is saying and showing that you are listening and understanding. You can use active listening to identify and remember the things that really get another excited, and to encourage them to share more with you. You can use active listening by nodding, making eye contact, paraphrasing, summarizing, or giving feedback. You can say "I see what you mean" or "That's amazing" or "I'm impressed by that."

Use feedback: This means giving a comment or a compliment that relates to the things that really get another excited, and that expresses your appreciation or admiration. You can use feedback to acknowledge and validate the other person's passions, and to make them feel good and valued. "That's awesome" or "That's very inspiring" or "You are so talented."

Creating excitement during conversations is crucial as it enhances engagement, stimulates emotions, and fosters a more impactful and memorable exchange.

43. Compliment Others

Compliments display that you are attentive, respectful, and appreciative of the other person. Complimenting others about what they are wearing, doing, or saying, makes them feel good and valued, and encourages them to continue the conversation.

Be specific: This means giving a compliment that is clear, precise, and relevant, and that focuses on a particular aspect of what the other person is wearing, doing, or saying. You can be specific by using descriptive words, examples, or comparisons. "I love your blue shirt. It brings out your eyes" or "You are doing an excellent job on this project. You have a lot of creativity and skill" or "You have a way with words. You always make me laugh."

Be sincere: This means giving a compliment that is honest, genuine, and heartfelt, and that reflects your true feelings and thoughts. You can be sincere using a positive tone, a smile, or eye contact, and avoiding exaggeration, sarcasm, or flattery. You can say "You look stunning today. I mean it" or "You are amazing at what you do. I really admire you" or "You are exceedingly kind. I appreciate you."

Be appropriate: This means giving a compliment that is suitable, respectful, and comfortable, and that matches the context, the relationship, and the culture. You can be appropriate using the right words, gestures, and timing, and avoiding any comments that might be offensive, intrusive, or embarrassing. "You have a beautiful smile. I hope you do not mind me saying that" or "You are very smart. I hope you are proud of yourself" or "You have a profound sense of style. I hope you do not think I am copying you."

Complimenting others during a conversation is valuable as it fosters positive emotions, enhances relationships, and boosts the recipient's self-esteem, contributing to a more enjoyable and constructive interaction.

44. Send Out Positive Signals

You are approachable, and pleasant. Sending out positive signals, makes others feel more comfortable, confident, and valued, and invite them to talk to you.

Smile: A smile is a universal sign of friendliness and warmth, and it can make you and others feel more relaxed and positive. A smile can convey your interest and enthusiasm and make others more receptive to your conversation. You can smile and say "Hello, I am Anna. It is nice to meet you."

Make eye contact: Eye contact is a way of showing your attention and respect to others, and it can signal your intention to start or continue a conversation. Eye contact can help you gauge others' interest and reaction and adjust your conversation accordingly. Make eye contact and say, "How are you today?" or "What do you think of this?"

Use a compliment: A compliment is a way of expressing your admiration or appreciation for something about others, such as their appearance, behavior, or achievement. A compliment can make others feel good and flattered, and more likely to respond positively to your conversation. Use a compliment and say "You have a beautiful voice. Do you sing?" or "You are very smart. What do you do?" or "You did an excellent job on that presentation. How did you prepare for it?"

Sending out positive signals during conversation is crucial as it enhances trust, fosters a positive atmosphere, and contributes to better understanding and rapport between individuals.

45. Talk to People You Enjoy

Trying to see and talk to people you enjoy, shows that you value and appreciate them. It will help you maintain and strengthen your relationships with them.

Schedule regular meetups: This is a way of ensuring that you have time and space to see and talk to people you enjoy, and it involves planning and arranging your meetings in advance. You can schedule regular meetups using a calendar, a phone, or a social media app, and choosing a convenient time, place, and frequency. "Let's have lunch every Friday" or "Let's go to the movies every month" or "Let's call each other every week."

Stay in touch in between meetups: This is a way of keeping the connection and communication with people you enjoy, and it involves sending messages, making calls, or sharing updates in between your meetings. You can stay in touch in between meetups using a text, an email, or a social media app, and sharing your thoughts, feelings, experiences, or interests. For example, you can say "How are you doing?" or "I saw this and thought of you" or "I miss you."

Show interest and support: This is a way of presenting your attention and care for people you enjoy, and it involves asking questions, giving feedback, or offering help or encouragement. You can express interest and support using words, tones, or gestures, and being empathetic, respectful, and positive. "What's new with you?" or "You are amazing" or "I'm here for you."

Engaging in conversations with people you enjoy fosters happiness, fulfills a basic human need for connection, and contributes to a sense of belonging and community.

46. How to Tell a Story

This is one way to tell a story, but not the only one. Diverse types of stories may require different approaches to storytelling. Stories may start with a hook or a twist that grabs the audience's attention, and then reveal the main point later. Other stories may use flashbacks, foreshadowing, or nonlinear structures to create suspense and intrigue. There is no single formula for how to tell a story effectively, but there are general tips and techniques that can help you improve your storytelling skills. Here are some ways to tell a better story.

Choose a clear central message: A remarkable story usually progresses towards a central moral or message. When crafting a story, you should have a definite idea of what you are building toward.

Embrace conflict: As a storyteller, you cannot shy away from conflict. Great storytellers craft narratives that have all sorts of obstacles and hardships strewn in the path of their protagonists. To be satisfied with a successful conclusion, audiences must watch the main characters struggle to achieve their goals.

Have a clear structure: There are diverse ways to structure a story, but the three ingredients a story must have been a beginning, middle, and end. On a more granular level, a successful story will start with an inciting incident, lead into rising action, build to a climax, and settle into a satisfying resolution.

Mine your subjective experiences: One of the best sources of inspiration for storytelling is your own life. You can draw from your memories, emotions, and insights to create stories that resonate with your audience. You can use your imagination to embellish or transform your experiences into fictional stories.

Engage your audience: A good storyteller knows how to captivate and connect with their audience. You can use various techniques to engage your audience, such as making eye contact, asking questions, using humor, gestures, and voice modulation, and adapting your story to the context and mood of the situation.

Observe good storytellers: One of the best ways to learn how to tell a story is to watch and listen to other storytellers. You can expose yourself to great storytellers in literature, film, podcasts, TED talks, and other media. You can observe how people around you tell stories in everyday conversations. Pay attention to how they use language, structure, emotion, and humor to convey their messages.

Being a good storyteller is essential for building trust, engaging audiences, and effectively conveying ideas.

47. Include Everyone in the Conversation

Including everyone in the group in conversation is a valuable skill that can foster a sense of belonging, respect, and collaboration among the participants. It can help you avoid awkward silences, conflicts, or misunderstandings. Here are tips on how to include everyone in the group in conversation whenever possible.

Be assertive and positive: A person who wants to include others must intentionally facilitate the conversation in a way that everyone in the group will enjoy. You can do this by being confident, and respectful in your tone and body language. You can use inclusive language, such as "we," "us," or "our," to create a sense of unity and involvement.

Make common connections: One of the easiest ways to include everyone in the conversation is to find topics that are relevant, interesting, or familiar to the group. You can do this by asking open-ended questions, sharing personal stories, or making references to current events, pop culture, or hobbies.

Keep the conversation going: A good conversationalist knows how to keep the conversation flowing and avoid dead ends. You can listen actively, showing interest, and giving feedback to the speakers. You can use transitions, follow-ups, or summaries to link the topics and move the conversation forward. You can invite others to share their opinions, experiences, or perspectives by using their names or eye contact.

Ask engaging questions: Asking questions is a powerful way to include everyone in the conversation and stimulate their curiosity and creativity. You can ask questions that are open-ended, specific, or provocative, depending on the purpose and tone of the conversation. You can ask questions that are relevant to the group's goals, interests, or challenges. You can use questions to clarify, challenge, or expand on the ideas that are discussed.

Listen: Listening is the most important skill for including everyone in the conversation. Listening shows that you care, respect, and value what others have to say. Listening helps you understand, learn, and empathize with others. Listening enables you to give appropriate and constructive feedback, suggestions, or solutions. To listen effectively, to pay attention, avoid distractions, and refrain from interrupting, judging, or dominating the conversation.

Inclusive conversations foster diverse perspectives, enhance understanding, and minimize conflicts, creating an environment where everyone feel valued and contributes effectively to the discourse.

48. Look for Signs of Boredom

Engaging your audience is crucial, but how do you know if your captivating story is landing? While rapt attention is ideal, it is not always the reality. Recognizing signs of boredom can help you adjust your approach and keep the conversation or presentation flowing. Here are three key areas to observe.

Body language: This is your silent language decoder. Crossed arms, fidgeting, glazed eyes, or frequent glances at the clock are all red flags. A slouching posture or leaning away can indicate waning attention.

Verbal cues: Listen beyond the words. Short, monosyllabic responses, frequent interruptions, or a lack of follow-up questions could signal disengagement. Yawns, sighs, or even forced laughter can be subtle indicators.

Engagement level: Observe the overall energy. Are they leaning in, taking notes, or actively participating? Do they ask clarifying questions or offer their own insights? A lack of these interactive elements can suggest the message is not resonating.

Remember, boredom is not always your fault. External factors like fatigue or distractions can play a role. However, acknowledging these signs allows you to adapt your approach. Here are a few tips.

Inject variety: Break up your monologue with questions, anecdotes, or multimedia elements.

Shift gears: Change the pace, tone, or even the topic to rekindle excitement.

Interactive elements: Encourage participation through polls, Q&A sessions, or group activities.

Humor and relatability: A well-timed joke or a relatable story can instantly pull your audience back in.

Being mindful of these signs and adjusting your approach, transforms potential boredom into active engagement, ensuring your message resonates and leaves a lasting impact.

49. Prepare Ahead of Time

Preparing ahead of time for each social or business function can help you make a good impression, achieve your goals, and enjoy the event. Here are tips on how to prepare for diverse types of functions.

For a social function, such as a party, a dinner, or a wedding, you should.

RSVP as soon as possible and confirm the date, time, location, dress code, and any other details of the event.

Research the host, the guests, and the occasion, and think of conversation topics or icebreakers that are appropriate and relevant.

Plan your outfit, accessories, and grooming, and make sure they suit the tone and style of the event.

Bring a gift, a card, or a thank-you note for the host, and express your appreciation for their invitation and hospitality.

Arrive on time, mingle with the guests, and follow the etiquette and customs of the event.

Have fun, but do not overindulge in food, drinks, or activities that could compromise your reputation or safety.

Leave at a reasonable time and follow up with the host and the guests after the event to thank them and maintain the connection.

For a business function, such as a meeting, a conference, or a presentation, try this.

Set a clear objective and agenda for the function and communicate it to the participants in advance.

Prepare the necessary materials, such as documents, slides, handouts, or equipment, and evaluate them before the function.

Research the background, and expectations of the participants, and tailor your content and delivery to suit their needs and preferences.

Dress professionally, confidently, and appropriately for the function, and pay attention to your body language and voice.

Arrive early, greet the participants, and introduce yourself and your role.

Stick to the agenda, engage the participants, and address any questions or feedback.

Summarize the main points, outcomes, and action items of the function, and thank the participants for their time and contribution.

Follow up with the participants after the function to provide any additional information, resources, or support.

Preparing for conversations is crucial as it enhances clarity and enables individuals to reflect on their intentions and goals, contributing to positive outcomes and successful interactions.

50. A Guide to Effective Communication

In conclusion, "ChatBuilder:Crafting Engaging Conversations from Scratch." has endeavored to unravel the intricacies of meaningful dialogue and equip readers with the tools necessary to engage in impactful conversations.

Throughout this book, we have explored various facets of effective communication, focusing on the art of initiating, maintaining, and concluding conversations.

As we wrap up this journey, it is imperative to reiterate the importance of active listening. The foundation of successful communication lies in listening attentively, understanding perspectives, and fostering empathy.

Additionally, cultivating adaptability has emerged as a significant aspect of engaging in diverse conversations, allowing individuals to navigate varying contexts with ease and flexibility.

Moreover, this book has highlighted the significance of authenticity in conversations. Authenticity fosters genuine connections and enhances the overall quality of interactions.

 Being true to oneself and embracing vulnerability, creates deeper connections and fosters trust in their conversations.

In the journey towards mastering conversations, continual practice and reflection are essential.

Each conversation serves as an opportunity for growth and refinement, allowing individuals to apply the principles outlined in this book to their real-life interactions.

"ChatBuilder: Crafting Engaging Conversations from Scratch." aims to inspire readers to become adept communicators, fostering meaningful connections and positively impacting their personal and professional lives.

All the amazing images in this book are the result of AI image generation in *Microsoft Designer*©

About the Author

Engineer by day and AI hobbyist by night. Loren possesses over 20 years of experience as a molding engineer specializing in the production of human implantable parts within prominent Biomedical Companies. His educational background includes a Bachelor of Science in Mechanical Engineering and a Master's degree in Manufacturing Systems from the University of Minnesota, along with a Master's in Regulatory Affairs and Services from St. Cloud State University. Additionally, Loren is a Certified Post-Secondary Teacher having completed certification from Bethel University.

His expertise extends to teaching opportunities, seeking roles in lectureships and adjunct faculty positions. Loren's teaching competencies lie in science, technology, and engineering, emphasizing Online Teaching, Collaboration and Problem Solving.

Loren is an author known for writing books on diverse topics, highlighting expertise in communication, persuasion, and success strategies.

Investigating AI and its uses is one of Loren's favorite hobbies. This book is a result of his passion for AI.
Loren can be found on the internet:

https://www.linkedin.com/in/lorenevers/
https://www.amazon.com/author/lorenevers/

www.ingramcontent.com/pod-product-compliance
Lightning Source LLC
Chambersburg PA
CBHW052054150726

48002CB00002B/889